EVERY DAY Matters

2025 Diary

A Year of Inspiration for the Mind, Body and Spirit

Created by
Jess Sharp
as seen on Instagram
@jessrachelsharp

WATKINS
Sharing Wisdom
Since 1893

Every Day Matters 2025 Diary

First published in UK and USA in 2024 by
Watkins, an imprint of Watkins Media Limited
Unit 11, Shepperton House
89–93 Shepperton Road
London N1 3DF

enquiries@watkinspublishing.com

Designed by Watkins Media Limited

Commissioning Editor: Lucy Carroll
Project Editor: Brittany Willis
Illustrator and Author: Jess Sharp
Head of Design: Karen Smith
Designer: Sneha Alexander

Desk Diary ISBN: 978-178678-834-4
Pocket Diary ISBN: 978-178678-833-7

Printed in China

Signs of the Zodiac:

♒ Aquarius	January 19–February 17
♓ Pisces	February 18–March 19
♈ Aries	March 20–April 18
♉ Taurus	April 19–May 19
♊ Gemini	May 20–June 20
♋ Cancer	June 21–July 21
♌ Leo	July 22–August 21
♍ Virgo	August 22–September 21
♎ Libra	September 22–October 22
♏ Scorpio	October 23–November 21
♐ Sagittarius	November 22–December 20
♑ Capricorn	December 21–January 19

Phases of the Moon:

- ● New moon
- ☽ First quarter
- ○ Full moon
- ☾ Last quarter

Abbreviations:

BCE: Before Common Era (equivalent of BC)
CE: Common Era (equivalent of AD)
UK: United Kingdom
SCO: Scotland
NIR: Northern Ireland
ROI: Republic of Ireland
CAN: Canada
USA: United States of America
NZ: New Zealand
AUS: Australia
ACT: Australian Capital Territory
NSW: New South Wales
NT: Northern Territory
QLD: Queensland
SA: South Australia
TAS: Tasmania
VIC: Victoria
WA: Western Australia

Publisher's Notes:

All dates relating to the zodiac signs and the
phases of the moon are based on Greenwich
Mean Time (GMT).

All North American holiday dates are based
on Eastern Standard Time (EST).

Jewish and Islamic holidays begin at sundown
on the date given. Islamic holidays may vary by
a day or two, as the Islamic calendar is based on
a combination of actual sightings of the moon
and astronomical calculations.

Dates were correct at the time of going to press.

2024

JANUARY
M	TU	W	TH	F	SA	SU
1	2	3	4	5	6	7
8	9	10	11	12	13	14
15	16	17	18	19	20	21
22	23	24	25	26	27	28
29	30	31				

FEBRUARY
M	TU	W	TH	F	SA	SU
			1	2	3	4
5	6	7	8	9	10	11
12	13	14	15	16	17	18
19	20	21	22	23	24	25
26	27	28	29			

MARCH
M	TU	W	TH	F	SA	SU
				1	2	3
4	5	6	7	8	9	10
11	12	13	14	15	16	17
18	19	20	21	22	23	24
25	26	27	28	29	30	31

APRIL
M	TU	W	TH	F	SA	SU
1	2	3	4	5	6	7
8	9	10	11	12	13	14
15	16	17	18	19	20	21
22	23	24	25	26	27	28
29	30					

MAY
M	TU	W	TH	F	SA	SU
		1	2	3	4	5
6	7	8	9	10	11	12
13	14	15	16	17	18	19
20	21	22	23	24	25	26
27	28	29	30	31		

JUNE
M	TU	W	TH	F	SA	SU
					1	2
3	4	5	6	7	8	9
10	11	12	13	14	15	16
17	18	19	20	21	22	23
24	25	26	27	28	29	30

JULY
M	TU	W	TH	F	SA	SU
1	2	3	4	5	6	7
8	9	10	11	12	13	14
15	16	17	18	19	20	21
22	23	24	25	26	27	28
29	30	31				

AUGUST
M	TU	W	TH	F	SA	SU
			1	2	3	4
5	6	7	8	9	10	11
12	13	14	15	16	17	18
19	20	21	22	23	24	25
26	27	28	29	30	31	

SEPTEMBER
M	TU	W	TH	F	SA	SU
						1
2	3	4	5	6	7	8
9	10	11	12	13	14	15
16	17	18	19	20	21	22
23	24	25	26	27	28	29
30						

OCTOBER
M	TU	W	TH	F	SA	SU
	1	2	3	4	5	6
7	8	9	10	11	12	13
14	15	16	17	18	19	20
21	22	23	24	25	26	27
28	29	30	31			

NOVEMBER
M	TU	W	TH	F	SA	SU
				1	2	3
4	5	6	7	8	9	10
11	12	13	14	15	16	17
18	19	20	21	22	23	24
25	26	27	28	29	30	

DECEMBER
M	TU	W	TH	F	SA	SU
						1
2	3	4	5	6	7	8
9	10	11	12	13	14	15
16	17	18	19	20	21	22
23	24	25	26	27	28	29
30	31					

2025

JANUARY
M	TU	W	TH	F	SA	SU
		1	2	3	4	5
6	7	8	9	10	11	12
13	14	15	16	17	18	19
20	21	22	23	24	25	26
27	28	29	30	31		

FEBRUARY
M	TU	W	TH	F	SA	SU
					1	2
3	4	5	6	7	8	9
10	11	12	13	14	15	16
17	18	19	20	21	22	23
24	25	26	27	28		

MARCH
M	TU	W	TH	F	SA	SU
					1	2
3	4	5	6	7	8	9
10	11	12	13	14	15	16
17	18	19	20	21	22	23
24	25	26	27	28	29	30
31						

APRIL
M	TU	W	TH	F	SA	SU
	1	2	3	4	5	6
7	8	9	10	11	12	13
14	15	16	17	18	19	20
21	22	23	24	25	26	27
28	29	30				

MAY
M	TU	W	TH	F	SA	SU
			1	2	3	4
5	6	7	8	9	10	11
12	13	14	15	16	17	18
19	20	21	22	23	24	25
26	27	28	29	30	31	

JUNE
M	TU	W	TH	F	SA	SU
						1
2	3	4	5	6	7	8
9	10	11	12	13	14	15
16	17	18	19	20	21	22
23	24	25	26	27	28	29
30						

JULY
M	TU	W	TH	F	SA	SU
	1	2	3	4	5	6
7	8	9	10	11	12	13
14	15	16	17	18	19	20
21	22	23	24	25	26	27
28	29	30	31			

AUGUST
M	TU	W	TH	F	SA	SU
				1	2	3
4	5	6	7	8	9	10
11	12	13	14	15	16	17
18	19	20	21	22	23	24
25	26	27	28	29	30	31

SEPTEMBER
M	TU	W	TH	F	SA	SU
1	2	3	4	5	6	7
8	9	10	11	12	13	14
15	16	17	18	19	20	21
22	23	24	25	26	27	28
29	30					

OCTOBER
M	TU	W	TH	F	SA	SU
		1	2	3	4	5
6	7	8	9	10	11	12
13	14	15	16	17	18	19
20	21	22	23	24	25	26
27	28	29	30	31		

NOVEMBER
M	TU	W	TH	F	SA	SU
					1	2
3	4	5	6	7	8	9
10	11	12	13	14	15	16
17	18	19	20	21	22	23
24	25	26	27	28	29	30

DECEMBER
M	TU	W	TH	F	SA	SU
1	2	3	4	5	6	7
8	9	10	11	12	13	14
15	16	17	18	19	20	21
22	23	24	25	26	27	28
29	30	31				

2026

JANUARY
M	TU	W	TH	F	SA	SU
			1	2	3	4
5	6	7	8	9	10	11
12	13	14	15	16	17	18
19	20	21	22	23	24	25
26	27	28	29	30	31	

FEBRUARY
M	TU	W	TH	F	SA	SU
						1
2	3	4	5	6	7	8
9	10	11	12	13	14	15
16	17	18	19	20	21	22
23	24	25	26	27	28	

MARCH
M	TU	W	TH	F	SA	SU
						1
2	3	4	5	6	7	8
9	10	11	12	13	14	15
16	17	18	19	20	21	22
23	24	25	26	27	28	29
30	31					

APRIL
M	TU	W	TH	F	SA	SU
		1	2	3	4	5
6	7	8	9	10	11	12
13	14	15	16	17	18	19
20	21	22	23	24	25	26
27	28	29	30			

MAY
M	TU	W	TH	F	SA	SU
				1	2	3
4	5	6	7	8	9	10
11	12	13	14	15	16	17
18	19	20	21	22	23	24
25	26	27	28	29	30	31

JUNE
M	TU	W	TH	F	SA	SU
1	2	3	4	5	6	7
8	9	10	11	12	13	14
15	16	17	18	19	20	21
22	23	24	25	26	27	28
29	30					

JULY
M	TU	W	TH	F	SA	SU
		1	2	3	4	5
6	7	8	9	10	11	12
13	14	15	16	17	18	19
20	21	22	23	24	25	26
27	28	29	30	31		

AUGUST
M	TU	W	TH	F	SA	SU
					1	2
3	4	5	6	7	8	9
10	11	12	13	14	15	16
17	18	19	20	21	22	23
24	25	26	27	28	29	30
31						

SEPTEMBER
M	TU	W	TH	F	SA	SU
	1	2	3	4	5	6
7	8	9	10	11	12	13
14	15	16	17	18	19	20
21	22	23	24	25	26	27
28	29	30				

OCTOBER
M	TU	W	TH	F	SA	SU
			1	2	3	4
5	6	7	8	9	10	11
12	13	14	15	16	17	18
19	20	21	22	23	24	25
26	27	28	29	30	31	

NOVEMBER
M	TU	W	TH	F	SA	SU
						1
2	3	4	5	6	7	8
9	10	11	12	13	14	15
16	17	18	19	20	21	22
23	24	25	26	27	28	29
30						

DECEMBER
M	TU	W	TH	F	SA	SU
	1	2	3	4	5	6
7	8	9	10	11	12	13
14	15	16	17	18	19	20
21	22	23	24	25	26	27
28	29	30	31			

2025 International Public Holidays

Argentina	Jan 1, Mar 3–4, Mar 24, Apr 2, Apr 18, May 1, May 25, Jun 16, Jun 20, Jul 9, Aug 18, Oct 13, Nov 17, Dec 8, Dec 25
Australia	Jan 1, Jan 27, Mar 3 (WA), Mar 10 (SA, VIC, ACT, TAS), Apr 18, Apr 19 (exc TAS, WA), Apr 20 (exc NT, SA, TAS), Apr 21, Apr 25, May 5 (NT, QLD), Jun 2 (WA, ACT), Jun 9 (exc QLD, WA), Oct 6 (ACT, NSW, QLD, SA), Dec 25–26
Austria	Jan 1, Jan 6, Apr 21, May 1, May 29, Jun 9, Jun 19, Aug 15, Oct 26, Nov 1, Dec 8, Dec 25–26
Belgium	Jan 1, Apr 21, May 1, May 29, Jun 9, Jul 21, Aug 15, Nov 1, Nov 11, Dec 25
Brazil	Jan 1, Apr 21, May 1, Sep 7, Oct 12, Nov 2, Nov 15, Dec 25
Canada	Jan 1, Apr 18, May 19 (exc NS, PEI, QC), July 1, Sep 1, Oct 13 (exc NS, PEI), Nov 11 (exc MB, NS, ON, QC), Dec 25, Dec 26 (AB, NB, NL, NT, NU, ON)
China	Jan 1, Jan 28–Feb 3, Apr 4, May 1–2, May 31–Jun 2, Oct 1–7, Oct 6
Denmark	Jan 1, Apr 17–18, Apr 20–21, May 29, Jun 8–9, Dec 25–26
Finland	Jan 1, Jan 6, Apr 18, Apr 20–21, May 1, May 29, Jun 8, Jun 20–21, Nov 1, Dec 6, Dec 24–26
France	Jan 1, Apr 18, Apr 21, May 1, May 8, May 29, Jun 8–9, Jul 14, Aug 15, Nov 1, Nov 11, Dec 25–26
Germany	Jan 1, Apr 18, Apr 21, May 1, May 29, Jun 9, Oct 3, Dec 25–26
Greece	Jan 1, Jan 6, Mar 3, Mar 25, Apr 18, Apr 20–21, May 1, Jun 8–9, Aug 15, Oct 28, Dec 25–26
India	Jan 1, Jan 26, Feb 26, Mar 14, Mar 31, Apr 14, Apr 18, Jun 7, Jul 6, Aug 15, Aug 16, Sep 5, Oct 2, Oct 21, Nov 5, Dec 25
Indonesia	Jan 1, Jan 27, Jan 29, Mar 29, Mar 31, Apr 1, Apr 18, May 1, May 12, May 29, Jun 1, Jun 7, Jun 27, Aug 17, Sep 5, Dec 25
Israel	Apr 13, Apr 19, May 1, Jun 2, Sep 23–24, Oct 2, Oct 7, Oct 14
Italy	Jan 1, Jan 6, Apr 20–21, Apr 25, May 1, Jun 2, Aug 15, Nov 1, Dec 8, Dec 25–26
Japan	Jan 1, Jan 13, Feb 11, Feb 23–24, Mar 21, Apr 29, May 3–5, Jul 21, Aug 11, Sep 15, Sept 23, Oct 13, Nov 3, Nov 23–24

Luxembourg	Jan 1, Apr 21, May 1, May 9, May 29, Jun 9, Jun 23, Aug 15, Nov 1, Dec 25–26
Mexico	Jan 1, Feb 3, Mar 17, May 1, Sep 16, Nov 17, Dec 25
Netherlands	Jan 1, Apr 18, Apr 20–21, Apr 27, May 5, May 29, Jun 8–9, Dec 25–26
New Zealand	Jan 1–2, Jan 20, Jan 27, Feb 3, Feb 6, Mar 10, Mar 24, Apr 18, Apr 21–22, Apr 25, Jun 2, Jun 20, Sep 22, Oct 24, Oct 27, Nov 3, Nov 14, Dec 1, Dec 25–26
Nigeria	Jan 1, Mar 30–31, Apr 18, Apr 21, May 1, Jun 6–7, Jun 12, Sep 4, Oct 1, Dec 25–26
Pakistan	Feb 5, Mar 23, Mar 31, Apr 1–2, May 1, Jun 7–8, Jul 5–6, Aug 14, Sep 5, Dec 25
Poland	Jan 1, Jan 6, Apr 20–21, May 1, May 3, Jun 8, Jun 19, Aug 15, Nov 1, Nov 11, Dec 25–26
Portugal	Jan 1, Apr 18, Apr 20, Apr 25, May 1, Jun 10, Jun 19, Aug 15, Oct 5, Nov 1, Dec 1, Dec 8, Dec 25
Republic of Ireland	Jan 1, Feb 3, Mar 17, Apr 21, May 5, Jun 2, Aug 4, Oct 27, Dec 25–26
Russia	Jan 1–7, Feb 23–24, Mar 8, Mar 10, May 1, May 9, Jun 12, Nov 4
South Africa	Jan 1, Mar 21, Apr 18, Apr 21, Apr 27–28, May 1, Jun 16, Aug 9, Sep 24, Dec 16, Dec 25–26
Spain	Jan 1, Jan 6, Apr 17 (exc Catalonia, Valencia), Apr 18, May 1, Aug 15, Oct 12, Nov 1, Dec 6, Dec 8 (exc Ceuta), Dec 25
Sweden	Jan 1, Jan 6, Apr 18, Apr 20–21, May 1, May 29, Jun 6, Jun 8, Jun 21, Nov 1, Dec 25–26
Turkey	Jan 1, Mar 30–Apr 1, Apr 23, May 1, May 19, Jun 6–9, Jul 15, Aug 30, Oct 29
United Kingdom	Jan 1, Jan 2 (SCO), Mar 17 (NI), Apr 18, Apr 21 (exc SCO), May 5, May 26, Jul 14 (NI), Aug 4 (SCO), Aug 25 (exc SCO), Dec 1 (SCO), Dec 25–26
United States	Jan 1, Jan 20, Feb 17, May 26, Jun 19, Jul 4, Sep 1, Oct 13, Nov 11, Nov 27, Dec 25

All information taken from publicholidays.com or timeanddate.com (US only).

WELCOME TO 2025!

Hello! How has the past year been for you? Whatever happened, I hope you showed yourself the grace and care you deserve as you navigated it all. And that you give yourself the gift of self-compassion in the year ahead.

With lots of space to organize your weeks, this diary focuses on a positive theme each month. It will help you to delve into your thoughts and feelings as the days go by. This year's themes include Beginnings, Patience, Nurture, Growth, Developing, Simplicity, Bloom, Self-Belief, Seasons, Letting Go, Clarity and Strength. Within each month you will find inspiring weekly quotes and prompts to support you in getting the most from the year. There are also creative activities such as drawing, for example, to use as a prompt. Sometimes working in a different way can lead to breakthroughs!

My wish is that this diary will help you to lean into everything the coming months have to offer, and that it will allow you a bit of quiet time to reflect. So, here's to 2025, a year filled with potential and possibilities, adventures and memories!

JANUARY

BEGINNINGS

As certain as endings are in life, so are beginnings.
Sometimes welcome, sometimes not so welcome,
beginnings are part of the natural order of things,
and while they may occasionally be difficult, they
can offer such possibility and hope.

If we look to nature, we can see new beginnings happen
all the time. As the seasons change, each brings with it a
new way of being, a new way of surviving. There is great
comfort to be found in this, in knowing that nothing is
ever permanent. It is even more comforting to remember
that we often have a choice and can make changes
ourselves, as well as embrace them when they occur
naturally. Nature doesn't fight as the leaves begin to fall
or unfurl; it knows that all things have their time and
place, and everything always changes.

How do you feel about beginnings? In the weeks ahead,
delve deeper and discover what new beginnings could
mean for you.

AFFIRMATION OF THE MONTH

I embrace the possibility
of beginning again

DEC 30 – JAN 5
BEGINNINGS

30 / MONDAY

31 / TUESDAY
New Year's Eve

1 / WEDNESDAY
New Year's Day
Kwanzaa ends

NOTES

> ## "When you arise in the morning give thanks for the food and for the joy of living."
>
> TECUMSEH (1768–1813), SHAWNEE CHIEF AND WARRIOR

2 / THURSDAY
Last day of Hanukkah
Public Holiday (SCO, NZ)

_____

_____

_____

_____

_____

_____

_____

_____

_____

_____

3 / FRIDAY

_____

_____

_____

_____

_____

_____

_____

_____

_____

_____

4 / SATURDAY

_____

_____

_____

_____

5 / SUNDAY
Twelfth Night

_____

_____

_____

_____

_____

_____

THINGS I'M GRATEFUL FOR

What better way to start afresh than to take stock of everything that you are grateful for? This week, turn to the Inspired Journalling section at the back of the diary and write a list of all the things you are grateful for. When you have a challenging day, use this list as a reminder that life isn't always as bad as we imagine.

6 / MONDAY ☽
Epiphany

7 / TUESDAY
Christmas Day (Orthodox)

8 / WEDNESDAY

NOTES

> ## "Every new beginning comes from some other beginning's end."
>
> SENECA THE YOUNGER (c. 4 BCE–65 CE), ROMAN PHILOSOPHER

9 / THURSDAY

_____
_____
_____
_____
_____
_____
_____
_____
_____
_____

10 / FRIDAY

_____
_____
_____
_____
_____
_____
_____
_____
_____
_____

11 / SATURDAY

_____
_____
_____
_____

12 / SUNDAY

_____
_____
_____
_____
_____

BEGIN IN EACH MOMENT

Each moment contains the potential for a new beginning. This week, think about any new beginnings happening in your life right now. How do you feel about them? What is ending for these new beginnings to get underway? What potential can you see in this moment?

JAN 13 – JAN 19
BEGINNINGS

13 / MONDAY ○

14 / TUESDAY
New Year's Day (Orthodox)

15 / WEDNESDAY

NOTES

> ## "And now we welcome the new year, full of things that have never been."
>
> RAINER MARIA RILKE (1875–1926), POET AND NOVELIST

16 / THURSDAY

17 / FRIDAY

18 / SATURDAY

19 / SUNDAY ≋
World Religion Day

MOVE FORWARD

Sometimes it can be nice to look back on the past. Other times, it can be completely okay to want to leave things there and start again. This week, think about something you'd like to leave firmly behind you and why. What did you learn from this experience? Is this insight something you can take with you into a new beginning?

JAN 20 – JAN 26
BEGINNINGS

20 / MONDAY
Martin Luther King Day
Inauguration Day (USA)

21 / TUESDAY ☾

22 / WEDNESDAY

NOTES

> "A journey of a thousand miles begins with a single step."
>
> LAO TZU (c. 5TH CENTURY BCE), TAOIST PHILOSOPHER

23 / THURSDAY

24 / FRIDAY

25 / SATURDAY
Burns Night (SCO)

26 / SUNDAY
Australia Day

START SOMETHING NEW

Think of a habit you'd like to have or something new you'd like to begin. It could be learning to knit or finding a moment to read each day. This week, find the time for it, even if just for a few minutes each day. As the weeks go by, stick with this activity and soon you will have developed a new skill or life-enhancing habit.

JANUARY OVERVIEW

M	TU	W	TH	F	SA	SU
30	31	1	2	3	4	5
6	7	8	9	10	11	12
13	14	15	16	17	18	19
20	21	22	23	24	25	26
27	28	29	30	31	1	2

this month I am grateful for . . .

REFLECTIONS ON BEGINNINGS

At the start of this new year, how do you feel about this new beginning?

_____

_____

_____

_____

Do you think you handle new beginnings well, or is change something you struggle with? Why?

_____

_____

_____

_____

_____

Sit and breathe. Now draw your breath as a line, moving your pencil up and down with each inhale and exhale, soaking up the relaxing motion in this moment of calm.

FEBRUARY

PATIENCE

Modern life can feel fast-paced and busy. With instant access to TV on demand, same-day courier deliveries and emails on our phones, we no longer have to wait for the things we once did. All of which has its benefits, but in this instant world of ours, the emphasis on patience has been lost a little.

Yet it's still important to remember the art of being patient. Wonderful things can sometimes take time. Self-development and healing aren't an instant process. Lessons can be learned when we linger; there is often such beauty to be found in the patient waiting. It gives us time to pause, reflect and re-evaluate our lives. To respond rather than react. To find the space to breathe.

How will you practice patience this month? Take your time in the coming days to reflect and discover what slowing down could offer you.

AFFIRMATION OF THE MONTH

Life is easier when I am patient

JAN 27 – FEB 2

PATIENCE

27 / MONDAY
International Holocaust
Remembrance Day

28 / TUESDAY

29 / WEDNESDAY ●
Chinese New Year
(Year of the Snake)

NOTES

> *"Patience attracts happiness;*
> *it brings near that which is far."*

SWAHILI PROVERB

30 / THURSDAY

_____

_____

_____

_____

_____

_____

_____

_____

_____

_____

_____

31 / FRIDAY

_____

_____

_____

_____

_____

_____

_____

_____

_____

_____

_____

1 / SATURDAY

St Brigid's Day (Imbolc)
Black History Month begins
(USA, CAN)

_____

_____

_____

_____

2 / SUNDAY

Groundhog Day
Candlemas

_____

_____

_____

_____

_____

BE PATIENT WITH YOURSELF

Ringing phones, pinging emails and everyday
noise can lead to a sensory overload that
hinders our ability to be patient. This week,
actively try to mute them for a small amount
of time each day. Perhaps turn off your phone
while you enjoy a quiet lunch and breathe in
the silence. See how this makes you feel.

FEB 3 – FEB 9

PATIENCE

3 / MONDAY	4 / TUESDAY	5 / WEDNESDAY ☽

NOTES

> *"Adopt the pace of nature. Her secret is patience."*
>
> RALPH W. EMERSON (1803–1882), AMERICAN ESSAYIST

6 / THURSDAY
Waitangi Day

7 / FRIDAY

8 / SATURDAY

9 / SUNDAY

WEATHER FEELINGS PATIENTLY

Sometimes we try to push away uncomfortable emotions, but this often just leads to us feeling worse. One way to tackle this is to view feelings as being like the weather. Storms will come but they will always pass. So let your feelings come; patiently experience them and allow them to move on when they are ready.

FEB 10 – FEB 16
PATIENCE

10 / MONDAY	11 / TUESDAY	12 / WEDNESDAY ○
		Abraham Lincoln's birthday

NOTES

> ## "The two most powerful warriors are patience and time."
>
> LEO TOLSTOY (1828–1910), RUSSIAN NOVELIST

13 / THURSDAY

_____
_____
_____
_____
_____
_____

14 / FRIDAY
St Valentine's Day

_____
_____
_____
_____
_____

15 / SATURDAY
Nirvana Day

_____
_____
_____
_____

16 / SUNDAY

_____
_____
_____
_____
_____

PERFECT YOUR PATIENCE

This week, spend some time thinking about a period in the past when you had to practice patience. Did you find it difficult? Why? Would you tackle anything differently should it happen again? Being able to recognize the way you handled the situation can be a great tool to help you navigate similar events in the future.

FEB 17 – FEB 23
PATIENCE

17 / MONDAY
Presidents' Day

18 / TUESDAY ♓

19 / WEDNESDAY

NOTES

"Patience is the best remedy for every trouble."

PLAUTUS (c. 254–184 BCE), ROMAN PLAYWRIGHT

20 / THURSDAY ☾

_____

_____

_____

_____

_____

_____

_____

_____

_____

_____

21 / FRIDAY

_____

_____

_____

_____

_____

_____

_____

_____

_____

_____

22 / SATURDAY

_____

_____

_____

_____

23 / SUNDAY

_____

_____

_____

_____

_____

OFFER AND RECEIVE PATIENCE

Patience is a wonderful gift to give and receive. To be patient with another soul and offer them your quiet support for as long as they need it can make such a difference. With this in mind, think about a time when someone showed you patience. How did it make you feel? Perhaps let them know how appreciative you were.

FEBRUARY OVERVIEW

M	TU	W	TH	F	SA	SU
27	28	29	30	31	1	2
3	4	5	6	7	8	9
10	11	12	13	14	15	16
17	18	19	20	21	22	23
24	25	26	27	28	1	2

this month I am grateful for . . .

_____

_____

_____

_____

_____

_____

_____

REFLECTIONS ON PATIENCE

How have you felt while concentrating on being more patient this month?

_____

_____

_____

_____

In what ways could being more patient benefit yourself and others?

_____

_____

_____

_____

_____

In the space below, write down one alternative response you can practice when you next feel impatient.

MARCH

NURTURE

We can often become so busy or caught up in nurturing others and making sure they are okay that we forget we deserve some care and attention too. When was the last time you did something that nurtured you? When did you last indulge in an activity that you love or that fulfils you?

Nurturing yourself may be at the bottom of your to-do list and seem unimportant, but this couldn't be further from the truth. Self-care and tending to your own wants and needs are integral to leading a fulfilled and happy life. Allowing ourselves time and space for the things that bring us joy, listening to our own needs and tuning in to what makes our body and soul sing are all essential for nurturing our physical and mental health.

This month, focus on what you need in order to nurture yourself and others – and why this is so important.

AFFIRMATION OF THE MONTH

I deserve to nurture
my body and my soul

FEB 24 – MAR 2
NURTURE

24 / MONDAY

25 / TUESDAY

26 / WEDNESDAY
Maha Shivaratri

NOTES

"Nurture your minds with great thoughts. To believe in the heroic makes heroes."

BENJAMIN DISRAELI (1804–1881), BRITISH STATESMAN AND WRITER

27 / THURSDAY

_____
_____
_____
_____
_____
_____
_____
_____
_____
_____

28 / FRIDAY ●
Ramadan begins at sundown

_____
_____
_____
_____
_____
_____
_____
_____
_____
_____

1 / SATURDAY
St David's Day

_____
_____
_____
_____

2 / SUNDAY

_____
_____
_____
_____
_____
_____

FEED YOUR SOUL

We may need to be reminded to nurture ourselves. This week, turn to the Inspired Journalling section at the back of the diary and make a list of all the things that bring you comfort and help to feed your soul. Turn to the list whenever you need inspiration for some nurturing self-love and self-care.

MAR 3 – MAR 9
NURTURE

3 / MONDAY

4 / TUESDAY
Shrove Tuesday

5 / WEDNESDAY
Ash Wednesday

NOTES

"My best friend is the one who brings out the best in me."

HENRY FORD (1863–1947), AMERICAN INDUSTRIALIST

6 / THURSDAY ☽
World Book Day

7 / FRIDAY

8 / SATURDAY
International Women's Day

9 / SUNDAY
Daylight Saving Time starts
(USA, CAN)

TEND TO YOUR RELATIONSHIPS

We can often take our relationships for granted, but every relationship needs nurturing. This week, think about one relationship in particular and write about a way in which that person lifts you up, a way in which they support you and a way in which they accept you. Afterwards, find the time to let the person know.

MAR 10 – MAR 16
NURTURE

10 / MONDAY
Commonwealth Day

11 / TUESDAY

12 / WEDNESDAY

NOTES

> ## "Dream as if you'll live forever. Live as if you'll die today."
>
> JAMES DEAN (1931–1955), AMERICAN ACTOR

13 / THURSDAY
Purim begins at sundown

14 / FRIDAY ○
Holi (Festival of Colours)

15 / SATURDAY

16 / SUNDAY

NURTURE YOUR DREAMS

Dreams can come true. This week, think about a dream you have for your life and what it looks like. Every day, add an extra detail to this dream. What would accomplishing it look like? How would it make a difference to you if it came true? The more you nurture your dream, the more you open your heart to it becoming a reality.

MAR 17 – MAR 23

NURTURE

17 / MONDAY
St Patrick's Day

18 / TUESDAY

19 / WEDNESDAY

NOTES

> **"Above all, do not forget your duty to love yourself."**
>
> SØREN KIERKEGAARD (1813–1855), DANISH PHILOSOPHER

20 / THURSDAY ♈︎
Spring Equinox (UK, ROI, USA, CAN)
Autumn Equinox (AUS, NZ)

_____

_____

_____

_____

_____

_____

_____

_____

21 / FRIDAY

_____

_____

_____

_____

_____

_____

_____

_____

22 / SATURDAY ☾

_____

_____

_____

_____

23 / SUNDAY

_____

_____

_____

_____

SHOW YOURSELF LOVE

Loving and nurturing ourselves can feel often difficult, but it's important for our emotional wellbeing. This week, smile at yourself in the mirror and think of the things you like about yourself. It may seem hard at first, but the more you practice, the more you will start to believe the words you say and the easier it becomes.

MAR 24 – MAR 30

NURTURE

24 / MONDAY

25 / TUESDAY

26 / WEDNESDAY

NOTES

"We don't stop playing because we grow old; we grow old because we stop playing."

GEORGE BERNARD SHAW (1856–1950), IRISH PLAYWRIGHT

27 / THURSDAY
Laylatul Qadr
(Night of Power)

28 / FRIDAY

29 / SATURDAY ●
Ramadan ends at sundown

30 / SUNDAY
Mother's Day (UK)
Eid al-Fitr begins at sundown
Daylight Saving Time
starts (UK)
British Summer Time begins

NURTURE YOUR INNER CHILD

This week, when you find yourself leaning toward negative self-talk, picture yourself as a small child, sitting on the bed. Instead of all the harsh words you've been saying to yourself, think about what you would say to your childhood self. What kind and loving words would you say to this little person? Is this what you need to hear now, too?

MARCH OVERVIEW

M	TU	W	TH	F	SA	SU
24	25	26	27	28	1	2
3	4	5	6	7	8	9
10	11	12	13	14	15	16
17	18	19	20	21	22	23
24	25	26	27	28	29	30
31	1	2	3	4	5	6

This month I am grateful for . . .

_____
_____
_____
_____
_____
_____
_____

REFLECTIONS ON NURTURE

In what ways have you made more time to nurture yourself this month?

_____

_____

_____

_____

_____

Has nurturing yourself made a difference to how you feel?

_____

_____

_____

_____

_____

Below or on a piece of paper, draw or write a decorative reminder that you too deserve love and compassion. Keep this as a reminder to nurture yourself more often.

GROWTH

Growth isn't always easy. It can be uncomfortable and confusing, but more often than not, the challenging times are those that teach us the most. As difficult as they are to navigate, the positive is that we can always learn from them. Every single experience, good or bad, shapes us and helps us to grow, whether we notice this or not.

Life can sometimes seem incredibly hard and unfair, but as long as we can trust in our own resilience, strength and self-compassion, we can remind ourselves that it won't be this way forever and we can keep going. The path of growth will lead us somewhere worthwhile, however long it takes, and hopefully that knowledge can help make any growing pains we feel a little more bearable.

AFFIRMATION OF THE MONTH

This growth is taking me somewhere worthwhile

MAR 31 – APR 6

GROWTH

31 / MONDAY

1 / TUESDAY
April Fools' Day

2 / WEDNESDAY

NOTES

> "Just as the heart becomes carefree in a place of green, growing plants, goodwill and kindness are born when our souls enter happiness."

RUMI (1207–1273), PERSIAN POET

3 / THURSDAY

4 / FRIDAY

5 / SATURDAY ☽

6 / SUNDAY

GROW YOUR GOOD THOUGHTS

Negative self-talk can be a barrier to growth. While self-belief and self-love are often difficult to practice, they are essential to how we carry ourselves through life. The next time you hear that negative inner voice, tell yourself that it isn't stating facts and is just a part of your mind that is trying to trick you.

APR 7 – APR 13
GROWTH

7 / MONDAY	8 / TUESDAY	9 / WEDNESDAY

NOTES

> "It does not matter how slowly you go
> so long as you do not stop."

CONFUCIUS (c. 551–479 BCE), CHINESE PHILOSOPHER

10 / THURSDAY

11 / FRIDAY

12 / SATURDAY
Passover begins at sundown

13 / SUNDAY ○
Palm Sunday

FOCUS ON HOW FAR YOU'VE COME

Growth can be such a slow process that we sometimes lose sight of how far we have already come. This week, think of something you are certain about today but were uncertain about a year ago. Did you join a club to meet new people? Leave a job that was making you unhappy? Recognize that growth and celebrate it!

APR 14 – APR 20
GROWTH

14 / MONDAY

15 / TUESDAY

16 / WEDNESDAY

NOTES

> "Intellectual growth should commence at birth and cease only at death."

ALBERT EINSTEIN (1879–1955), GERMAN PHYSICIST

17 / THURSDAY
Maundy Thursday

18 / FRIDAY
Good Friday
Good Friday (Orthodox)

19 / SATURDAY ♉
Easter Saturday
Easter Saturday (Orthodox)
Passover ends at sundown

20 / SUNDAY
Easter Sunday
Easter (Orthodox)

GROW YOUR KNOWLEDGE

There is never an end to learning. This week, focus on growing your knowledge and learning more about something you're passionate about. Search the internet for podcasts, online lectures and experts in the field. Dive right in and soak it all up. Then, why not share what you've learned with a loved one?

APR 21 – APR 27
GROWTH

21 / MONDAY ☾
Easter Monday
Easter Monday (Orthodox)

22 / TUESDAY
Earth Day

23 / WEDNESDAY
St George's Day

NOTES

> ## "The tree of silence bears the fruit of peace."
> ARABIC PROVERB

24 / THURSDAY

25 / FRIDAY
Anzac Day

26 / SATURDAY

27 / SUNDAY ●

EMBRACE THE QUIET TIMES

Sometimes the most growth can take place in our quiet, reflective moments. Spend an hour this week without any distractions. Sit quietly and just do nothing. Let your mind wander where it needs to and reflect on anything that comes up. Allow yourself to just be with your inner self. Ideally, do this more than once!

APRIL OVERVIEW

M	TU	W	TH	F	SA	SU
31	1	2	3	4	5	6
7	8	9	10	11	12	13
14	15	16	17	18	19	20
21	22	23	24	25	26	27
28	29	30	1	2	3	4

This month I am grateful for . . .

_____

_____

_____

_____

_____

_____

_____

_____

_____

REFLECTIONS ON GROWTH

Has thinking about growth led you to realize more about yourself in ways you hadn't done before?

_____

_____

_____

_____

_____

Do you think you have grown in the past month? How?

_____

_____

_____

_____

_____

Draw three flowers. Write a negative thought in one and a positive alternative in the next. In the third, jot down evidence supporting the positive statement. How can reframing your thoughts help inner growth?

MAY

DEVELOPING

Growth leads to development. We are always developing, sometimes slowly and quietly, sometimes in leaps and bounds brought on by events. We may not even realize the changes in ourselves. Think back to five years ago: are you the same person now as you were then? Do you have the same views? Would you react in the same way to problems and challenges?

Our development can be helped or hindered by many different things. Who we choose to spend our time with and how we spend our time can both be massive influences. Our development can also be shaped by whether we are fully honest with ourselves when we reflect on past experiences and habits, and whether we feel safe and secure enough to be authentic with ourselves in the present moment too! The experiences we gather as we move through life all play their part and feed into the tapestry of who we are and who we are becoming.

AFFIRMATION OF THE MONTH

I am developing into the best person I can be

APR 28 – MAY 4
DEVELOPING

28 / MONDAY

29 / TUESDAY

30 / WEDNESDAY

NOTES

"Don't let the fear of striking out hold you back."

BABE RUTH (1895–1948), AMERICAN BASEBALL PLAYER

1 / THURSDAY
Beltane

2 / FRIDAY

3 / SATURDAY

4 / SUNDAY ☽

TAKE TINY STEPS

If we get stuck in a routine, stepping out of our comfort zone can feel scary. But it can often be a great way of pushing ourselves and developing emotionally. It's okay to take this process slowly, step by tiny step. Every little experience feeds into who you are becoming. Give something new a go and see how it feels.

MAY 5 – MAY 11

DEVELOPING

5 / MONDAY
Early May Bank Holiday
(UK, ROI)
Cinco de Mayo

6 / TUESDAY

7 / WEDNESDAY

NOTES

> "Develop success from failures. Discouragement and failure are two of the surest stepping stones to success."

DALE CARNEGIE (1888–1955), AMERICAN WRITER AND LECTURER

8 / THURSDAY

_____
_____
_____
_____
_____
_____
_____
_____
_____
_____
_____

9 / FRIDAY

_____
_____
_____
_____
_____
_____
_____
_____
_____
_____
_____

10 / SATURDAY

_____
_____
_____
_____

11 / SUNDAY

Mother's Day (USA, CAN, AUS, NZ)

_____
_____
_____
_____
_____

DEVELOP THROUGH EXPERIENCE

This week, think of an experience that you found difficult. Make a list of everything you learned from it and how it's helped you develop as a person. Keep this list as a reminder that no matter how hard things may seem, you are more than capable of navigating your way through any hurdles that life throws at you.

MAY 12 – MAY 18

DEVELOPING

12 / MONDAY ○
Vesak Day (Buddha Day)

13 / TUESDAY

14 / WEDNESDAY

NOTES

"If adventures will not befall a young lady in her own village, she must seek them abroad."

JANE AUSTEN (1775–1817), ENGLISH NOVELIST

15 / THURSDAY

16 / FRIDAY

17 / SATURDAY

18 / SUNDAY

SEEK OUT THE NEW

A great way to carry on developing is to keep embracing and seeking out new experiences. This week, turn to the Inspired Journalling section at the back of the diary and write a list of all the places you'd like to visit. Anywhere at all, near or far! When planning your next adventure, turn to this list as inspiration.

MAY 19 – MAY 25

DEVELOPING

19 / MONDAY
Victoria Day (CAN,
exc NS, NU, QC)

20 / TUESDAY ☾ ♊

21 / WEDNESDAY

NOTES

> "The highest reward for one's toil is not what one gets for it, but what one becomes by it."

JOHN RUSKIN (1819–1900), BRITISH POLYMATH

22 / THURSDAY

_____
_____
_____
_____
_____
_____
_____
_____
_____
_____
_____

23 / FRIDAY

_____
_____
_____
_____
_____
_____
_____
_____
_____
_____
_____

24 / SATURDAY

_____
_____
_____
_____

25 / SUNDAY

_____
_____
_____
_____
_____
_____

DEVELOP YOUR MINDSET

We can sense that it's time for a change in life when things no longer feel aligned for us. However, this can be hard to admit and even harder to put into action. This week, identify an area of your life that, if changed slightly, could help you to develop and thrive more. Is there a way you could gently implement that change?

MAY OVERVIEW

M	TU	W	TH	F	SA	SU
28	29	30	1	2	3	4
5	6	7	8	9	10	11
12	13	14	15	16	17	18
19	20	21	22	23	24	25
26	27	28	29	30	31	1

This month I am grateful for . . .

_____

_____

_____

_____

_____

_____

_____

_____

REFLECTIONS ON DEVELOPING

How has it felt to reflect on the ways you've developed throughout your life?

_____

_____

_____

_____

_____

In what ways will you seek out more opportunities for development in the future?

_____

_____

_____

_____

_____

Sketch a picture of yourself in the past, as you are now and how you might look in the future. Do these snapshots offer any insights into how you can develop with time?

SIMPLICITY

Sometimes, life can feel like a constant treadmill, with task after task. This is why it is so important to find time for simple pleasures in among all that hustle and bustle. Whether it be taking a more scenic route home and pausing to breathe in the fresh air, or enjoying a cup of tea with a friend, there is so much comfort to be found in the simple things and so much beauty to enjoy in them.

Contrary to how it seems a lot of the world works, you do not always have to be moving forward and striving for more. You do not have to hustle every day. It is possible to be perfectly happy with a simple life, embracing the peace that comes with this. Sometimes real progress can mean realizing this and becoming completely content with the simplicity of standing still and taking a moment to soak it all in for a while.

AFFIRMATION OF THE MONTH

I am slowing down and enjoying the simple moments

MAY 26 – JUN 1
SIMPLICITY

26 / MONDAY
Spring Bank Holiday (UK)
Memorial Day (USA)

27 / TUESDAY ●

28 / WEDNESDAY

NOTES

> "Simplicity is the most difficult thing to secure in this world; it is the last limit of experience and the last effort of genius."

GEORGE SAND (1804–1876), FRENCH NOVELIST

29 / THURSDAY
Ascension Day

_____
_____
_____
_____
_____
_____
_____
_____
_____
_____
_____

30 / FRIDAY

_____
_____
_____
_____
_____
_____
_____
_____
_____
_____
_____

31 / SATURDAY

_____
_____
_____
_____
_____

1 / SUNDAY

_____
_____
_____
_____
_____

FIND BALANCE IN SIMPLICITY

When our lives are hectic, we forget to prioritize the important things. Think about the last 24 hours. How much time have you spent doing what you have to do, rather than what you'd like to do? What commitments drain you? Could you simplify your days to allow more time for moments you can cherish?

JUN 2 – JUN 8
SIMPLICITY

2 / MONDAY

3 / TUESDAY ☽

4 / WEDNESDAY

NOTES

> ## "If you try to please all, you please none."
>
> AESOP (c. 620–564 BCE), GREEK FABULIST

5 / THURSDAY

_____

_____

_____

_____

_____

_____

_____

_____

_____

6 / FRIDAY
Eid al-Adha (Feast of the
Sacrifice) begins at sundown

_____

_____

_____

_____

_____

_____

_____

_____

_____

7 / SATURDAY

_____

_____

_____

_____

8 / SUNDAY
Pentecost (Whit Sunday)

_____

_____

_____

_____

_____

SIMPLIFY YOUR LIFE WITH BOUNDARIES

Saying no can be very hard, especially if by
nature you are a people pleaser. This week,
try to implement a boundary and say no to
something you do not want or have to do.
"No" is a complete sentence and can be said
kindly. Sometimes saying no to others makes
it simpler to say yes to ourselves.

SIMPLICITY

9 / MONDAY
Whit Monday

10 / TUESDAY

11 / WEDNESDAY ○

NOTES

"Simplicity is the ultimate sophistication."

LEONARDO DA VINCI (1452–1519), ITALIAN POLYMATH

12 / THURSDAY

_____
_____
_____
_____
_____
_____
_____
_____
_____
_____

13 / FRIDAY

_____
_____
_____
_____
_____
_____
_____
_____
_____
_____

14 / SATURDAY

_____
_____
_____
_____
_____

15 / SUNDAY

Trinity Sunday
Father's Day (UK, ROI, USA, CAN)

_____
_____
_____
_____

ENJOY SIMPLE PLEASURES

Simple pleasures make life a little bit sweeter. They do not have to be big or grand; all they have to do is warm our souls. Think about one thing that brings you pleasure. Whether it's spending time with a loved one or enjoying a cosy night in with a good film, this week make time to indulge yourself in that simple pleasure.

JUN 16 – JUN 22
SIMPLICITY

16 / MONDAY

17 / TUESDAY
King's Birthday Parade
(Trooping the Colour)

18 / WEDNESDAY ☾

NOTES

> "Have nothing in your houses that you do not know to be useful or believe to be beautiful."

WILLIAM MORRIS (1834–1896), BRITISH DESIGNER, AUTHOR AND ARTIST

19 / THURSDAY
Corpus Christi
Juneteenth (USA)

_____

_____

_____

_____

_____

_____

_____

_____

20 / FRIDAY
Summer Solstice
(USA, CAN, UK, ROI)

_____

_____

_____

_____

_____

_____

_____

_____

21 / SATURDAY ♋
King's Birthday
Winter Solstice (AUS, NZ)

_____

_____

_____

_____

22 / SUNDAY

_____

_____

_____

_____

CLEAR YOUR SPACE AND YOUR MIND

Are you a clutter lover or do you prefer a stripped back way of living? If you tend toward a more cluttered way of life, spend time this week tackling a space in your home and simplifying it. Whether it is a whole room, a drawer or a wardrobe, give it a good once-over and get rid of everything you no longer need.

JUN 23 – JUN 29

SIMPLICITY

23 / MONDAY

24 / TUESDAY

25 / WEDNESDAY ●

NOTES

> "Simple pleasures are the last healthy refuge in a complex world."

OSCAR WILDE (1854–1900), IRISH AUTHOR AND PLAYWRIGHT

26 / THURSDAY
Islamic New Year
(first day of Muharram)
begins at sundown

27 / FRIDAY

28 / SATURDAY

29 / SUNDAY

SAVOUR THE SIMPLE MOMENTS

Some of life's most fulfilling moments are small and quiet. This week, note down one thing each day that fills up your heart. It could be listening to the birds sing in the morning, watching the sun set, enjoying that first cup of coffee as you rise. Whatever it is, no matter how small, take the time to appreciate its simple beauty.

JUNE OVERVIEW

M	TU	W	TH	F	SA	SU
26	27	28	29	30	31	1
2	3	4	5	6	7	8
9	10	11	12	13	14	15
16	17	18	19	20	21	22
23	24	25	26	27	28	29
30	1	2	3	4	5	6

This month I am grateful for . . .

_____
_____
_____
_____
_____
_____
_____
_____

REFLECTIONS ON SIMPLICITY

Has stripping back and thinking about the simple things been beneficial for you this month?

_____

_____

_____

_____

_____

How has concentrating on the little things felt?

_____

_____

_____

_____

_____

_____

Turn a simple scribble into a colourful creation. Doodle below or on a piece of paper, grab some pens or pencils and calmly colour in the gaps that the scribble has made.

JULY

BLOOM

The start of July marks the midpoint of the year. How has it been for you so far? Sometimes, when we are caught up in the busyness of day-to-day life, we can forget what it is that we love to do. We may lose touch with what fulfils our souls, feeds our lust for living and makes us bloom . . .

For some, this can be found in the healing arms of nature. For others, it may be in their paint pallet as they sit down to create art. It could be the connections you have with your family and loved ones, or the excitement you experience in exploring new places. Whatever it is that fills you up and helps you bloom, you can't go wrong by doing more of it.

Set aside time this month to find out what makes you bloom and then look at ways to bring more of this into your life during the rest of the year.

AFFIRMATION OF THE MONTH

I welcome that which makes me bloom into my life

JUN 30 – JUL 6
BLOOM

30 / MONDAY

1 / TUESDAY
Canada Day

2 / WEDNESDAY ☽

NOTES

> ## "If you look the right way, you can see that the whole world is a garden."
>
> FRANCES HODGSON BURNETT (1849–1924),
> BRITISH–AMERICAN NOVELIST AND PLAYWRIGHT

3 / THURSDAY

_____

_____

_____

_____

_____

_____

_____

_____

_____

_____

4 / FRIDAY
Independence Day (USA)

_____

_____

_____

_____

_____

_____

_____

_____

_____

_____

5 / SATURDAY

_____

_____

_____

_____

6 / SUNDAY

_____

_____

_____

_____

_____

BLOOM WITH JOY

What brings you joy and makes your soul bloom? This week, turn to the Inspired Journalling section at the back of the diary and write a list of everything that makes you bloom. Big or small, bold or seemingly insignificant, write it down and refer to it whenever you need a little reminder.

JUL 7 – JUL 13
BLOOM

7 / MONDAY	8 / TUESDAY	9 / WEDNESDAY

NOTES

> "Those who bring sunshine to the lives of others cannot keep it from themselves."

J. M. BARRIE (1860–1937), SCOTTISH NOVELIST AND PLAYWRIGHT

10 / THURSDAY ○

_____
_____
_____
_____
_____
_____
_____
_____
_____
_____

11 / FRIDAY

_____
_____
_____
_____
_____
_____
_____
_____
_____
_____

12 / SATURDAY
Battle of the Boyne (NI)

_____
_____
_____
_____

13 / SUNDAY

_____
_____
_____
_____
_____

LET YOUR LAUGHTER BLOOM

Nothing beats a good belly laugh! Laughter is good for connection, easing stress and helping us bloom. This week, seek out something that makes you laugh, whether this is a chat with a funny friend, a TV comedy or some hilarious videos on TikTok. Laughter is wonderful and you can never have too much of it.

JUL 14 – JUL 20
BLOOM

14 / MONDAY
Battle of the Boyne (NI)
observed

15 / TUESDAY

16 / WEDNESDAY

NOTES

> "There are always flowers for those who want to see them."

HENRI MATISSE (1869–1954), FRENCH ARTIST

17 / THURSDAY

18 / FRIDAY ☾

19 / SATURDAY

20 / SUNDAY

FREE YOURSELF FROM EXPECTATIONS

Our expectations of who we should be can sometimes prevent us from blooming into our happiest selves. Each morning this week, think about your expectations for the day. Pick a negative one and challenge it with this mantra: "Whatever happens, I will be okay and I will be happy!" Repeat this when you need the reminder.

JUL 21 – JUL 27

BLOOM

21 / MONDAY	22 / TUESDAY ♌	23 / WEDNESDAY

NOTES

> **"Every flower is a soul blossoming in nature."**
>
> GÉRARD DE NERVAL (1808–1855), FRENCH WRITER

24 / THURSDAY ●

25 / FRIDAY

26 / SATURDAY

27 / SUNDAY

REMINISCE ON WHEN YOU FELT MOST IN BLOOM

This week, think back over the past few months and pinpoint when you felt most in bloom. When did you feel like your most happy, authentic self? Why do you think that was? If you can work out what sparked this feeling, you can start to bring more of it into your life.

JULY OVERVIEW

M	TU	W	TH	F	SA	SU
30	1	2	3	4	5	6
7	8	9	10	11	12	13
14	15	16	17	18	19	20
21	22	23	24	25	26	27
28	29	30	31	1	2	3

This month I am grateful for . . .

_____
_____
_____
_____
_____
_____
_____
_____
_____
_____

REFLECTIONS ON BLOOM

How did it feel to concentrate on the things that make you bloom this month?

_____

_____

_____

_____

What can you bring into your life to help you bloom during the rest of the year?

_____

_____

_____

_____

_____

Photograph some of the things that you find beautiful and fill your soul. Turn these images into a collage to remind you of all the joys to be found in day-to-day life.

AUGUST

SELF-BELIEF

Do you believe in yourself? When we're used to being self-critical or have low self-esteem, believing in ourselves can feel alien to us. But if we can just practice some self-compassion and hold on to the facts, perhaps we will be able to achieve so much more and feel more fulfilled, too.

Healthy self-belief can lead us to try new things and experiences; it can push us out of our comfort zones to achieve those things we never thought we would. It can hold our hand as we navigate new ground and reassure us that we already have exactly what we need within us to make it through.

Self-belief is a wonderful tool that can help you achieve a fulfilled and happy life. If it's something that doesn't usually come naturally to you, I hope you will start believing in your own brilliance this month!

AFFIRMATION OF THE MONTH

I have all that I need inside to take a chance and try new things

JUL 28 – AUG 3

SELF–BELIEF

28 / MONDAY

29 / TUESDAY

30 / WEDNESDAY

NOTES

"Believe you can and you're halfway there."

THEODORE ROOSEVELT (1858–1919),
26TH PRESIDENT OF THE UNITED STATES

31 / THURSDAY

1 / FRIDAY ☽
Lughnasadh (Lammas)

2 / SATURDAY

_____

_____

_____

_____

_____

_____

3 / SUNDAY

_____

_____

_____

_____

_____

BELIEVE IN YOURSELF
Self-belief may be a tricky concept for some
of us, but honing in on what we love about
ourselves can really boost our confidence.
This week, turn to the Inspired Journalling
section at the back of this diary and make
a list of everything you love and like about
yourself – anything that makes you proud.

AUG 4 – AUG 10
SELF-BELIEF

4 / MONDAY
August Bank Holiday
(ROI, SCO)

5 / TUESDAY

6 / WEDNESDAY

NOTES

> ## "As soon as you trust yourself, you will know how to live."
>
> JOHANN WOLFGANG VON GOETHE (1749–1832), GERMAN POLYMATH

7 / THURSDAY

8 / FRIDAY

9 / SATURDAY ○

10 / SUNDAY

BE TRUE TO YOU

Sometimes other people's views of us can hold us back from fully believing in our own capabilities. This week, write a list of how you feel pigeonholed or limited by others' views of you. What small changes can you implement to help you break free from these limiting generalizations and feed your self-belief?

AUG 11 – AUG 17
SELF-BELIEF

11 / MONDAY

12 / TUESDAY

13 / WEDNESDAY

NOTES

> "Keep away from people who try to belittle your ambitions . . . the really great make you feel that you, too, can become great."

MARK TWAIN (1835–1910), AMERICAN WRITER

14 / THURSDAY

_____
_____
_____
_____
_____
_____
_____
_____
_____
_____
_____

15 / FRIDAY

_____
_____
_____
_____
_____
_____
_____
_____
_____
_____
_____

16 / SATURDAY ☾

_____
_____
_____
_____

17 / SUNDAY

_____
_____
_____
_____
_____

FIND YOUR PEOPLE

When we are surrounded by people who make us feel worse about ourselves, it can be hard to channel self-belief. People who encourage and praise us are those who allow us to become the best version of ourselves. Identify these people in your life. Can you quietly distance yourself from anybody who is not on that list?

AUG 18 – AUG 24
SELF-BELIEF

18 / MONDAY	19 / TUESDAY	20 / WEDNESDAY

NOTES

> ## "Fall in love with yourself, with life, and then with whoever you want."
>
> FRIDA KAHLO (1907–1954), MEXICAN ARTIST

21 / THURSDAY

22 / FRIDAY ♍

23 / SATURDAY ●

24 / SUNDAY

ACCEPT COMPLIMENTS

When people say nice things to us, it can be easy to dismiss this as flattery. This week, make a conscious effort to accept any compliments you receive. This will also help you recognize that the good things you hear about yourself are true. Remember them when your self-belief needs a boost.

AUG 25 – AUG 31

SELF-BELIEF

25 / MONDAY
Summer Bank Holiday
(UK exc SCO)

26 / TUESDAY

27 / WEDNESDAY

NOTES

> ## "Public opinion is a weak tyrant compared with our own private opinion."
>
> HENRY DAVID THOREAU (1817–1862),
> AMERICAN NATURALIST AND PHILOSOPHER

28 / THURSDAY

_____
_____
_____
_____
_____
_____

29 / FRIDAY

_____
_____
_____
_____
_____
_____

30 / SATURDAY

_____
_____
_____
_____

31 / SUNDAY ☽

_____
_____
_____
_____

CLEANSE YOUR SOCIAL MEDIA

It is important to ensure that our social media feeds are safe and friendly spaces. Anybody in our feeds who makes us feel inadequate can affect how we view ourselves. Spend time this week going through your apps and unfollow anyone who may be harming your self-belief. See how this new filtered feed makes you feel.

AUGUST OVERVIEW

M	TU	W	TH	F	SA	SU
28	29	30	31	1	2	3
4	5	6	7	8	9	10
11	12	13	14	15	16	17
18	19	20	21	22	23	24
25	26	27	28	29	30	31

This month I am grateful for . . .

REFLECTIONS ON SELF-BELIEF

How have you found concentrating on your own self-belief this month?

_____

_____

_____

_____

_____

Are there any areas of your life that you think would benefit if you had more self-belief?

_____

_____

_____

_____

_____

_____

Find or draw a picture of yourself as a small child. On it, write down how wonderful, capable and unique this little person is. Look at this whenever your self-belief needs a boost.

SEASONS

Like elsewhere in nature, nothing is constant in our lives. Everything changes and shifts. There will be times when things seem easier and happier, when we can feel ourselves blossoming and blooming. And there will be others when we really have to dig deep to find the energy to get through – and that's okay.

Life is full of ups and downs, of beautiful seasons and darker days. Think about the flowers. They are not always in bloom; they all have their time to grow, then fade. In autumn, the trees will lose their leaves. The seasons of our own lives aren't too dissimilar. Whatever our age, we will go through difficult times and lighter, more care-free days. We just have to treat ourselves with compassion and kindness as we navigate it all and trust that things are unfolding as they should. Remember that your now is never your forever.

AFFIRMATION OF THE MONTH

I have the resilience to handle all the seasons of my life

SEP 1 – SEP 7

SEASONS

1 / MONDAY
Labour Day (USA, CAN)

2 / TUESDAY

3 / WEDNESDAY

NOTES

> "To be interested in the changing seasons is a happier state of mind than to be hopelessly in love with spring."

GEORGE SANTAYANA (1863–1952), SPANISH–AMERICAN PHILOSOPHER

4 / THURSDAY
Milad un-Nabi (birthday of
the Prophet Muhammed)
begins at sundown

5 / FRIDAY

6 / SATURDAY

7 / SUNDAY ○
Father's Day (AUS, NZ)

WHAT SEASON ARE YOU IN

This week, spend a little time thinking about
the season of life that you're currently in. Is it a
comfortable one? Is it one of transition? Happy
or challenging? Consider how it's affecting you.
If you need to, can you get some support to
ease things a little? Remember that all seasons
change and you will not stay in this one forever.

SEP 8 – SEP 14

SEASONS

8 / MONDAY

9 / TUESDAY

10 / WEDNESDAY

NOTES

> "How many things by season season'd are,
> To their right praise and true perfection!"

WILLIAM SHAKESPEARE (1564–1616), ENGLISH PLAYWRIGHT AND POET

11 / THURSDAY

12 / FRIDAY

13 / SATURDAY

14 / SUNDAY ☾

GREET EACH SEASON

Seasons come and go. When you are next outside, look for the natural signs of the seasons – the trees, the plants, the weather. Think about the seasonal signs in your own life and where you'd like to be this time next year. Are there any steps you can take to make this potential season a reality?

SEP 15 – SEP 21

SEASONS

15 / MONDAY

16 / TUESDAY

17 / WEDNESDAY

NOTES

> "Moments like this are buds on the tree of life, flowers of darkness they are."

VIRGINIA WOOLF (1882–1941), ENGLISH WRITER

18 / THURSDAY

_____
_____
_____
_____
_____
_____
_____
_____
_____
_____

19 / FRIDAY

_____
_____
_____
_____
_____
_____
_____
_____
_____
_____

20 / SATURDAY

_____
_____
_____
_____

21 / SUNDAY ●
International Day of Peace

_____
_____
_____
_____
_____

TILL YOUR MIND

Each season brings new gardening tasks: tilling, weeding and pruning. There may be things on your mind, such as worries or to-do lists, which also need attention. This week, write down all your thoughts. The act of getting it out of your head and onto paper should show you how much you are carrying and help you feel lighter.

SEP 22 – SEP 28

SEASONS

22 / MONDAY ♎

Autumn Equinox (UK, ROI, USA, CAN)
Rosh Hashanah (Jewish New Year) begins at sundown

23 / TUESDAY

Spring Equinox (AUS, NZ)

24 / WEDNESDAY

NOTES

> "There are some things you learn best in calm, and some in storm."
>
> WILLA CATHER (1873–1947), AMERICAN NOVELIST

25 / THURSDAY

26 / FRIDAY

27 / SATURDAY

28 / SUNDAY

WRITE A LETTER TO YOUR PAST SELF

We face many ups and downs and different seasons over the years. This week, turn to the Inspired Journalling section at the back of the diary and write a letter to your past self about a difficult time you've experienced. Offer yourself the support you needed then and note how resilient you are for getting through it all.

SEPTEMBER OVERVIEW

M	TU	W	TH	F	SA	SU
1	2	3	4	5	6	7
8	9	10	11	12	13	14
15	16	17	18	19	20	21
22	23	24	25	26	27	28
29	30	1	2	3	4	5

This month I am grateful for . . .

REFLECTIONS ON SEASONS

What kind of season would you say you are in right now?

_____

_____

_____

_____

_____

How do you feel about being in this season?

_____

_____

_____

_____

_____

Draw a seasonal symbol of your life at the moment. It can be anything –
a snowflake, a flower, tumbling leaves. This may help you clarify your
feelings about where you currently are.

OCTOBER

LETTING GO

Letting go can be a wonderfully empowering experience – or an incredibly hard and upsetting step to take. Although it can feel difficult at times, there is little more freeing than letting go of the things that are no longer good for us or which are holding us back.

Acknowledging that something is no longer serving you and making the steps to remove it from your life can be very challenging to do, but it can also lead to an enormous sense of peace and wellbeing. Why keep carrying something that is weighing you down?

Of course, letting go requires self-awareness and recognition that these things are causing us pain or difficulties. This can often be tricky to come to terms with, or even recognize, but once that first hurdle is overcome we can work toward doing what is best for us and our wellbeing.

AFFIRMATION OF THE MONTH

I let go of the things that no longer serve me well

SEP 29 – OCT 5
LETTING GO

29 / MONDAY ☽

30 / TUESDAY

1 / WEDNESDAY
Black History Month
begins (UK)
Yom Kippur (Day of
Atonement) begins
at sundown

NOTES

> ## "All the art of living lies in a fine mingling of letting go and holding on."
>
> HAVELOCK ELLIS (1859–1939), ENGLISH PHYSICIAN AND WRITER

2 / THURSDAY

3 / FRIDAY

4 / SATURDAY

5 / SUNDAY

DON'T BE SO HARD ON YOURSELF

In today's digital age, we may feel we need to be accessible 24/7. This week, consider whether you could implement boundaries around this and let go of some of the demands that are placed on you. Maybe you could take emails off your phone? Or set a time limit with social media? See how setting these boundaries makes you feel.

OCT 6 – OCT 12
LETTING GO

6 / MONDAY
Sukkot (Feast of the
Tabernacles) begins
at sundown

7 / TUESDAY ○

8 / WEDNESDAY

NOTES

> ## "I can shake off everything as I write; my sorrows disappear, my courage is reborn."
>
> ANNE FRANK (1929–1945), GERMAN-BORN DIARIST

9 / THURSDAY

_____
_____
_____
_____
_____
_____
_____
_____
_____
_____
_____

10 / FRIDAY

_____
_____
_____
_____
_____
_____
_____
_____
_____
_____
_____

11 / SATURDAY

_____
_____
_____
_____

12 / SUNDAY

_____
_____
_____
_____
_____
_____

WRITE IT TO RELEASE IT

It's often hard to let go of negative emotions, as they can be buried deep within ourselves. The act of writing can be a great way to let go of whatever is weighing you down. This week, identify something negative that you are holding on to and write it down. Perhaps even screw it up and throw it away. Then see how you feel.

OCT 13 – OCT 19
LETTING GO

13 / MONDAY ☾
Indigenous Peoples' Day/
Columbus Day
Thanksgiving (CAN)
Sukkot ends at sundown
Shemini Atzeret begins
at sundown

14 / TUESDAY
Simchat Torah begins
at sundown

15 / WEDNESDAY

NOTES

> *"Shared joy is a double joy;*
> *shared sorrow is half a sorrow."*

SWEDISH PROVERB

16 / THURSDAY

17 / FRIDAY

18 / SATURDAY

19 / SUNDAY

TALK IT OUT

We often overthink the things that are bothering us, and torture ourselves by reliving the details in our head over and over again. This week, tell a person you trust about something that is weighing on your mind. Often, just getting it out in the open can mean an enormous burden is lifted.

OCT 20 – OCT 26
LETTING GO

20 / MONDAY
Diwali/Deepavali

21 / TUESDAY ●

22 / WEDNESDAY

NOTES

> "When one door closes, another opens; but we often look so long and so regretfully upon the closed door that we do not see the one which has opened for us."
>
> ALEXANDER GRAHAM BELL (1847–1922), SCOTTISH-BORN INVENTOR

23 / THURSDAY ♏

24 / FRIDAY

25 / SATURDAY

_____

26 / SUNDAY

British Summer Time ends
Daylight Saving Time ends
(UK)

FOCUS ON WHAT YOU CAN CONTROL

Feeling that you are not in control can cause anxiety. This week, think about what is making you anxious. Are there any practical steps you can take to relieve this feeling, or is this something you can't control? If so, repeat this affirmation to yourself: "I focus on what I can control and I let go of what I can't."

OCTOBER OVERVIEW

M	TU	W	TH	F	SA	SU
29	30	1	2	3	4	5
6	7	8	9	10	11	12
13	14	15	16	17	18	19
20	21	22	23	24	25	26
27	28	29	30	31	1	2

This month I am grateful for . . .

REFLECTIONS ON LETTING GO

How have you found focusing on letting go of difficult thoughts and feelings this month?

_____

_____

_____

_____

In what ways do you think letting go of things that weigh you down could help you?

_____

_____

_____

_____

_____

_____

Draw around both hands. On one hand, write down the things you wish to hold on to. On the other, write down the things you need to let go. Seeing it all written down can help you implement change.

Don't miss out on next year's diary! See the back page for details on how to order your copy

NOVEMBER

CLARITY

While it can be difficult to find clarity around how we're really feeling, and why we feel the way we do, unpacking our emotions can be hugely beneficial. Of course, sometimes emotions just are what they are. Other times, our feelings may be sending us important messages about ourselves, and getting some clarity around them can help us to work through them and move forward in our lives.

Maybe you know you're more susceptible to being oversensitive when you're tired. Or perhaps something made you cry because it reminded you of a moment from your past and triggered those feelings again. For example, could those occasional feelings of road rage really be down to your anxieties around driving? Being able to clarify what emotions we're feeling and the reasons behind these can aid our self-awareness and help us grow.

AFFIRMATION OF THE MONTH

I see my feelings with clarity and do not hide them from myself or others

27 / MONDAY

28 / TUESDAY

29 / WEDNESDAY ☽

NOTES

> "Clarity of mind means clarity of passion, too; this is why a great and clear mind loves ardently and sees distinctly what it loves."

BLAISE PASCAL (1623–1662), FRENCH PHILOSOPHER

30 / THURSDAY

31 / FRIDAY
Halloween

1 / SATURDAY
Samhain

2 / SUNDAY
Daylight Saving Time ends
(USA, CAN)

DESIGN YOUR PERFECT DAY

What would your perfect day look like – where you are at your happiest and most content? This week, write a little timeline of that perfect day, step by step. Who are you with? What would you do? By clarifying exactly what your most fulfilling and happy day looks like, you will be better placed to make it a reality.

NOV 3 – NOV 9

CLARITY

3 / MONDAY	4 / TUESDAY	5 / WEDNESDAY ○
		Guy Fawkes Day

NOTES

"Dwell not on the faults and shortcomings of others; instead, seek clarity about your own."

SIDDHARTHA GAUTAMA (c.5TH CENTURY BCE), FOUNDER OF BUDDHISM

6 / THURSDAY

7 / FRIDAY

8 / SATURDAY

9 / SUNDAY

COULD YOU DO THINGS DIFFERENTLY?

This week, take a moment at the end of each day to think about one thing you could do differently tomorrow that would benefit you and help you feel more positive and fulfilled. Then, try to implement it. At the end of the week, reflect on whether clarifying these small changes daily has helped your week go better.

NOV 10 – NOV 16

CLARITY

10 / MONDAY

_____

_____

_____

_____

_____

_____

_____

_____

_____

_____

_____

_____

_____

11 / TUESDAY

Remembrance Day
(CAN, UK)
Veterans Day (USA)

_____

_____

_____

_____

_____

_____

_____

_____

_____

_____

_____

_____

12 / WEDNESDAY ☾

_____

_____

_____

_____

_____

_____

_____

_____

_____

_____

_____

_____

NOTES

_____

_____

_____

> # "It is only with the heart that one can see rightly; what is essential is invisible to the eye."

ANTOINE DE SAINT-EXUPÉRY (1900–1944), FRENCH AUTHOR AND AVIATOR

13 / THURSDAY

14 / FRIDAY

15 / SATURDAY

16 / SUNDAY

WHAT DO YOU NEED RIGHT NOW?

Take a moment this week to reflect on how you feel and what it is that you need most right now. Is it to set aside some time for self-care? Do you need more sleep? Or to drop some of the plates you're spinning? Once you have clarified your inner needs, think about how you can potentially meet them and rectify any imbalance.

NOV 17 – NOV 23

CLARITY

17 / MONDAY

18 / TUESDAY

19 / WEDNESDAY

NOTES

"It is never too late to be what you might have been."

GEORGE ELIOT (1819–1880), ENGLISH NOVELIST

20 / THURSDAY ●   21 / FRIDAY   22 / SATURDAY ↗

World Hello Day

_____   _____   _____
_____   _____   _____
_____   _____   _____
_____   _____   _____
_____   _____

23 / SUNDAY

_____   _____   _____
_____   _____   _____
_____   _____   _____
_____   _____   _____

FIND A LIFE YOU LOVE

During this week, simply think about what you really love about life. What fills you up? What brings you joy? Who are your favourite people and why? Life can often get difficult, but being able to find clarity around these things and take comfort in them can help us navigate all roads and eventually lead us home.

NOV 24 – NOV 30
CLARITY

24 / MONDAY

25 / TUESDAY

26 / WEDNESDAY

NOTES

> **"If a man will begin with certainties, he shall end in doubts; but if he will be content to begin with doubts, he shall end in certainties."**
>
> FRANCIS BACON (1561–1626), ENGLISH PHILOSOPHER

27 / THURSDAY
Thanksgiving Day (USA)

28 / FRIDAY ☽
Black Friday

29 / SATURDAY

30 / SUNDAY
First Sunday of Advent
St Andrew's Day

WHAT DO YOU NEED TO CHANGE?

Whether it concerns a job, a relationship or a friendship, we may sometimes sense that change needs to occur but have trouble admitting it. This week, think about an aspect of your life and what you could do to transform it into something more. When you have some clarity around this, try to take the first step.

NOVEMBER OVERVIEW

M	TU	W	TH	F	SA	SU
27	28	29	30	31	1	2
3	4	5	6	7	8	9
10	11	12	13	14	15	16
17	18	19	20	21	22	23
24	25	26	27	28	29	30

This month I am grateful for . . .

_____
_____
_____
_____
_____
_____
_____
_____

REFLECTIONS ON CLARITY

In what ways have you sought clarity in your life this month?

_____

_____

_____

_____

_____

How has it felt to look more clearly at your emotions?

_____

_____

_____

_____

_____

_____

Draw a heart. In it, sketch or write down your feelings. Once you have
filled the space, think about what you would like to see more of in there.

DECEMBER

STRENGTH

Here we are, at the end of another year! How do you feel? Elated? Exhausted? Strength doesn't mean never showing emotion. It isn't about powering on regardless. It means being honest about how we feel, what we need and how we implement that in our lives.

True strength can mean admitting we're overwhelmed and taking the steps to lighten our load. It's knowing we might not be okay right now, but trusting we have faced similar mountains and heartache – and we can make it through again.

Strength shows up differently for different people. Sometimes we may not feel particularly strong, but it is important to trust that we are. Everything we have experienced and survived comes down to our unwavering inner strength. Even when we feel at our weakest, we can remind ourselves of all that we have overcome. Congratulate yourself on what you have learned about yourself this year, which makes you stronger than ever.

AFFIRMATION OF THE MONTH
I have more strength than I know

DEC 1 – DEC 7

STRENGTH

1 / MONDAY
St Andrew's Day observed
World AIDS Day
Cyber Monday

2 / TUESDAY

3 / WEDNESDAY

NOTES

> "Strength does not come from physical capacity. It comes from an indomitable will."

MAHATMA GANDHI (1869–1948), INDIAN SOCIAL REFORMER AND ACTIVIST

4 / THURSDAY ○

5 / FRIDAY

6 / SATURDAY

7 / SUNDAY

YOU GOT THROUGH IT!

You have exercised such strength to make it through this year and the difficulties it brought. Even when you felt like you couldn't go on, you did – and you made it! Your strength is astounding. This week, think of a time when you were struggling and commend yourself for getting through. You deserve to feel proud.

DEC 8 – DEC 14

STRENGTH

8 / MONDAY	9 / TUESDAY	10 / WEDNESDAY

NOTES

> "He who believes is strong; he who doubts is weak. Strong convictions precede great actions."
>
> LOUISA MAY ALCOTT (1832–1888), AMERICAN NOVELIST

11 / THURSDAY ☾

12 / FRIDAY

13 / SATURDAY

14 / SUNDAY

Hanukkah begins at sundown

STRENGTHEN YOUR ROUTINE

When times are hard, routines can be a saving grace that give us a sense of normality and the strength to cope. Do you have any set routines? Are there any changes you could make to them that would enhance your energy and mood? Work on improving your routine this week and see how this makes you feel.

DEC 15 – DEC 21

STRENGTH

15 / MONDAY

16 / TUESDAY

17 / WEDNESDAY

NOTES

> "You have power over your mind – not outside events. Realize this, and you will find strength."

MARCUS AURELIUS (121–180 CE),
ROMAN EMPEROR AND PHILOSOPHER

18 / THURSDAY

19 / FRIDAY

20 / SATURDAY ●

21 / SUNDAY ♑
Winter Solstice (UK, ROI, USA, CAN)

PRACTICE SELF-CARE

It is important to pause occasionally and make sure we are taking care of ourselves. Self-care helps us feel more capable and gives us the strength to continue. This week, take some time for yourself, whether it be a walk in nature, a coffee break or a therapy session. Allocate that time to regain your strength.

DEC 22 – DEC 28
STRENGTH

22 / MONDAY
Hanukkah ends at sundown
Summer Solstice (AUS, NZ)

23 / TUESDAY

24 / WEDNESDAY
Christmas Eve

NOTES

> "It is our attitude toward events, not events themselves, which we can control. Nothing is by its own nature calamitous . . ."

EPICTETUS (c. 50–135 CE), GREEK PHILOSOPHER

25 / THURSDAY
Christmas Day

_____
_____
_____
_____
_____
_____
_____
_____
_____
_____
_____

26 / FRIDAY
Boxing Day
Kwanzaa begins

_____
_____
_____
_____
_____
_____
_____
_____
_____
_____
_____

27 / SATURDAY ☽

_____
_____
_____
_____

28 / SUNDAY

_____
_____
_____
_____
_____
_____

FIND STRENGTH IN FACING YOUR FEARS

What's one thing you've always been scared to do? This week, see if you can find the strength to do it – whether it's telling someone how you feel, asking for a pay rise or wearing something you've not had the courage to wear. Once you've done it you'll almost certainly find more strength to tackle other niggling fears.

DEC 29 – JAN 4

STRENGTH

29 / MONDAY	30 / TUESDAY	31 / WEDNESDAY
		New Year's Eve

NOTES

> "Everyone has oceans to fly, if they have the heart to do it. Is it reckless? Maybe. But what do dreams know of boundaries?"

AMELIA EARHART (1897–1937), AMERICAN AVIATOR

1 / THURSDAY
New Year's Day
Kwanzaa ends

2 / FRIDAY

3 / SATURDAY

4 / SUNDAY

BE STRONG AND BUILD YOUR FUTURE

This week, spend some time thinking and dreaming about what you'd like to seek in your life if you had the courage. Would you love to change career or start a hobby? Research what this would entail and whether it is something that you could achieve in the year ahead. Can you make a plan to get this in motion?

DECEMBER OVERVIEW

M	TU	W	TH	F	SA	SU
1	2	3	4	5	6	7
8	9	10	11	12	13	14
15	16	17	18	19	20	21
22	23	24	25	26	27	28
29	30	31	1	2	3	4

This month I am grateful for . . .

REFLECTIONS ON STRENGTH

In what ways have you acknowledged your own strength this month?

_____

_____

_____

_____

_____

Do you think recognizing your own strengths could help you feel more prepared for the future?

_____

_____

_____

_____

_____

_____

_____

Draw a tree. On each leaf, draw or write down something that gives you strength in times of need – like an activity, song or person. Refer to your tree when you need a reminder.

INSPIRED JOURNALLING

The six journalling pages in this section are designed to help you reflect on some of the important things in life, and to make your year as fulfilling, supportive and enjoyable as possible. They each correspond to one of the monthly themes in the diary and are designed to give you space to create your own list or summary – of things that you are grateful for, ways to nurture yourself, places you'd like to visit, reminders of what brings you joy, reasons to celebrate yourself and sources of support when times are hard.

Use these spaces in whichever way works best for you by writing down as many or as few ideas as you can think of for each topic. The lists aren't meant to be set in stone: keep revisiting them and adding to them, and maybe even continue them elsewhere . . .

Things that I'm Grateful For

BEGINNINGS (JANUARY)

What better way to start the year than by reflecting on the things that you are grateful for? This is a wonderfully grounding activity and the perfect way to reframe your thinking into a more positive light. Focusing on what enhances your days and fills you up emotionally can also offer you some insight into what you perhaps need to incorporate more of in your life in the year ahead.

Use the space below to compile a list of all the things you are grateful for. What makes you feel happy, whole and contented? What makes you feel fulfilled? What gives you purpose?

Refer back to the list whenever you need to be reminded of the good things in life, or would like inspiration for what to fill more of your days with this year.

things that bring me comfort

NURTURE (MARCH)

Knowing and being able to call upon what you find comforting in times of stress can help you to develop and maintain a healthier relationship with your emotional wellbeing. Taking the time to get to know your own healthy coping mechanisms and means of self-soothing is such a valuable thing to do and a wonderful way to nurture yourself and your emotional health.

When you need nurturing, do you know what comforts and reassures you? Use this space to write down anything that helps you in times of difficulty. This could be anything from a walk in the fresh air, watching TV, crafting or reading, to having a nice relaxing bath, calling a loved one, having a duvet day or getting an early night. Whenever you need some ideas to help nurture yourself, refer back to this list.

places I'd Like to visit

DEVELOPING (MAY)

Experiencing new places is a wonderful way to widen your outlook and develop your personal growth. Getting away or visiting somewhere different, exploring an unfamiliar landscape, meeting new people and immersing yourself in fresh experiences can help you to expand your horizons and consider new ways of doing, being, speaking, understanding, and so much more . . .

With this in mind, use the space below to make a list of all the places that you'd like to visit, both in your own country and beyond. Anywhere at all! This could range from a new art gallery, to a whole continent. Refer back to this list when you have a free day or are in the position to take a longer trip away.

what brings me joy

BLOOM (JULY)

Knowing what lights you up and makes you happy is important. With this awareness, you will be able to see what is best for you and where to place your energy. You will know what to seek when times are difficult and which people and places can help you bloom. By concentrating on these things and opening yourself up to them, you will be better placed to create a fulfilling and uplifting life for yourself.

In the space below, write a list of all the things that help you to bloom into the best version of yourself – the activities, people and places that make you feel seen, heard and happy. When you are feeling a bit down or lost, look at this list to remind yourself of what you may need to get yourself back to full bloom again.

Things I Love About Me

SELF-BELIEF (AUGUST)

Our inner critic often does a great job of focusing on the negatives and amplifying our perceived failures. Comparing ourselves too often to others can mean we start to lose confidence. The only way we can change that habit and grow our self-belief is by offering ourselves some compassion and kindness.

Write down a list of everything you love about yourself and all the amazing things you have achieved in your life so far. It may feel a little awkward at first, but remember that no one else is going to read it. Praise yourself for anything you are proud of, and recall any compliments you've received, too. Celebrate your successes, however big or small. Refer back to this list when your self-belief is flagging; it will offer you the best pep talk you could have.

Letter to a strugging past self

SEASONS (SEPTEMBER)

Life is full of ups and downs, trials and tribulations. Along with the wonderful seasons in life, come the not-so-great ones. These more difficult and testing times can feel near impossible to deal with, but we draw on our strength and resilience to get through them.

Think of a particular time that was difficult for you – a time when you didn't think you'd make it through but you did. Picture yourself back then and write yourself a letter of support. What did you need to hear? What encouraging words can you offer? Not only will this show you how resilient and strong you are, but it's a wonderful testimony to have to hand in case you hit more turbulent times again. It can act as a letter to your past self and a potential letter of support to a future you, as well.

Notes From the Author

Hello, I'm Jess – a designer, illustrator and writer based in West Yorkshire, UK.

I run my Instagram page @jessrachelsharp, where I share gentle, positive reminders for when you might need them most. I also have my own line of stationery, enamel pins and gifts, which I sell from my website: www.jessrachelsharp.com. My hope is that my products can offer some support and encouragement through life's many ups and downs.

I began doing what I do after going through a bit of a tough time and attending therapy. I wanted to remember all the helpful words that I was hearing and the life-enhancing epiphanies that I was having, so I began to incorporate them into designs. I started posting them to my Instagram and I realized that not only were they helpful for me, but they resonated with others, too. And I haven't stopped since!

It has been an absolute dream to work with Watkins Publishing on putting these ideas into this diary. I hope you find it as uplifting and inspiring to read and use as I have found it to create.

We are constantly learning and growing on our journey through life, so I hope that this diary can offer some gentle guidance for you along the way – helping you to discover more about yourself and make the very most of each and every day.

Here's wishing you much love, hope and happiness for a fulfilling year ahead!

Jess xxx

Notes

Don't miss out on next year's diary!

To pre-order your 2026 *Every Day Matters Diary*
with FREE postage and packing,*
call our UK distributor on +44 (0)1206 255800.

*Free postage and packing for UK delivery addresses only. Offer limited to three books per order.

WATKINS
Sharing Wisdom
Since 1893

Our books celebrate conscious, passionate, wise and happy living.
Be part of the community by visiting
watkinspublishing.com

 WatkinsPublishing    @watkinswisdom

WatkinsPublishingLtd   +watkinspublishing1893